Introduction To Rhetorical Theory

15-Comm-3006-003 | Online Course

2021 Edition
University of Cincinnati
Professor Kristina Galyen

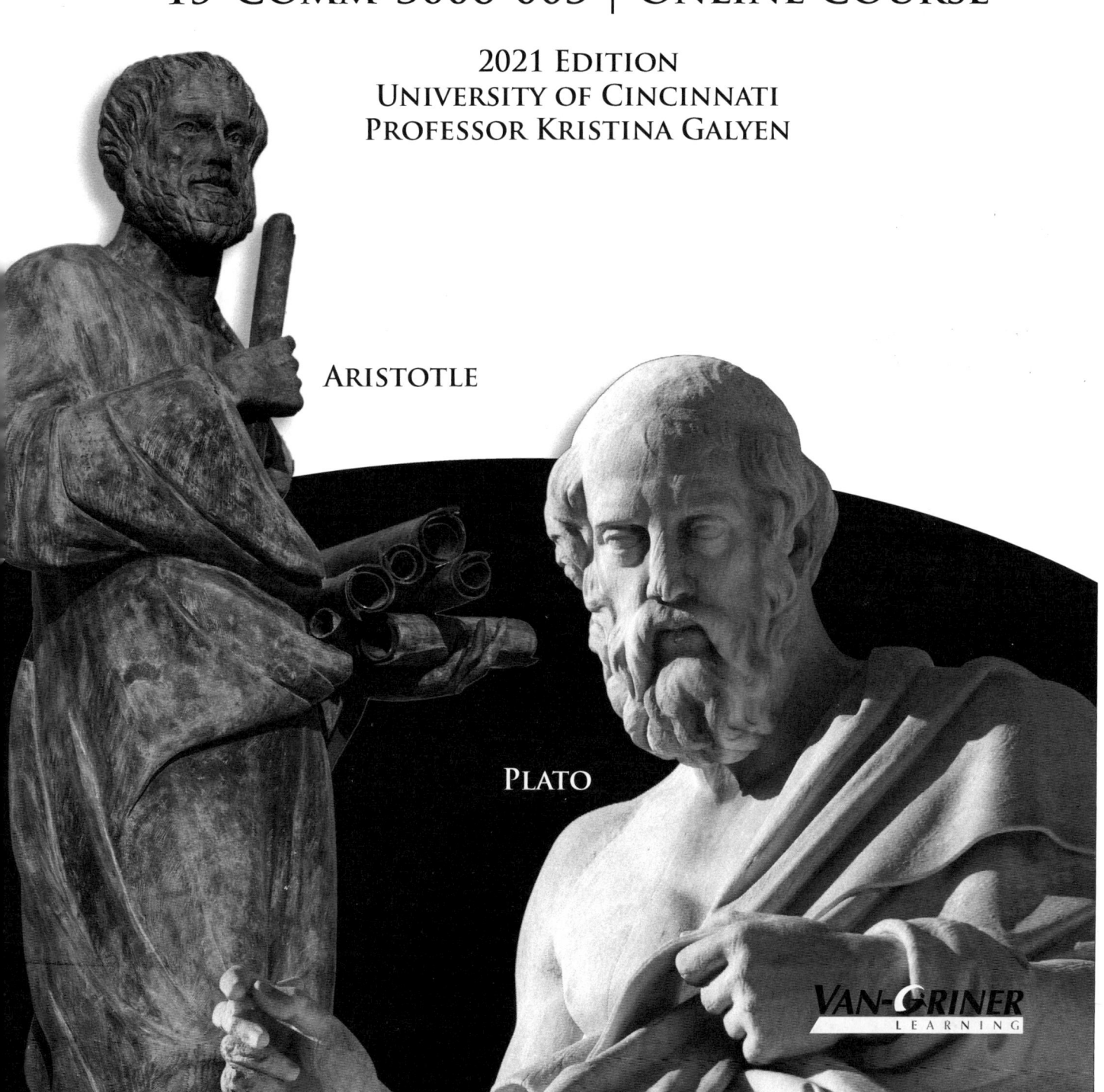

Aristotle

Plato

Introduction to Rhetorical Theory

15-COMM-3006-003 Online Course
2021 Edition
University of Cincinnati
Professor Kristina Galyen

Copyright © by Dr. Kristina Galyen
Copyright © by Van-Griner, LLC

Photos and other illustrations are owned by Van-Griner Learning or used under license.
All products used herein are for identification purposes only, and may be trademarks or registered trademarks of their respective owners.

All rights reserved. No part of this book may be reproduced or transmitted in any form or by any means, electronic or mechanical, including photocopying, recording or by any information storage and retrieval system, without written permission from the author and publisher.

Printed in the United States of America
10 9 8 7 6 5
ISBN: 978-1-61740-917-2

Van-Griner Learning
Cincinnati, Ohio
www.van-griner.com

President: Dreis Van Landuyt
Project Manager: Janelle Lange
Customer Care Lead: Lauren Wendel

Galyen 917-2 W20
317590-326105
Copyright © 2022

VAN-GRINER
LEARNING

TABLE OF CONTENTS

	GRID	2
	DEFINITIONS	9
	WHAT IS RHETORIC?	11
1|	AN OVERVIEW OF RHETORIC	15
2|	THE ORIGINS AND EARLY HISTORY OF RHETORIC	18
3|	PLATO VS. THE SOPHISTS: RHETORIC ON TRIAL	22
4|	ARISTOTLE ON RHETORIC	30
5|	RHETORIC AT ROME: CICERO	36
6|	RHETORIC IN CHRISTIAN EUROPE: ST. AUGUSTINE	38
9|	CONTEMPORARY RHETORIC I: ARGUMENT, AUDIENCES, AND ADVOCACY	40
10|	CONTEMPORARY RHETORIC II: KENNETH BURKE	42
11|	CONTEMPORARY RHETORIC III: TEXTS, POWER, AND ALTERNATIVES	60

GRID: THE THREE ELEMENTS OF RHETORICAL THEORY

	ONTOLOGY	EPISTEMOLOGY	AXIOLOGY
Sophists			
Plato			
Aristotle			
Cicero			
Augustine			
Habermas			

Grid

	ONTOLOGY	EPISTEMOLOGY	AXIOLOGY
Burke			
Bitzer			
Vatz			
Narratives			
Weaver			
Feminism Critique			

DEFINITIONS: THEORIST'S DEFINITIONS OF RHETORIC

KNOW EVERY DEFINITION

- Department of Communication:

- Herrick:

- Sophists:

- Plato:

- Aristotle:

- Cicero:

- Augustine:

- Habermas:

INTRODUCTION TO RHETORICAL THEORY

- Burke:

- Bitzer:

- Vatz:

- Bahktin:

- Bormann:

- Weaver:

- Feminism Critique:

WHAT IS RHETORIC? LECTURE

SUPPLEMENTAL OUTLINE: NOT FOUND IN TEXT

I. Definitions

    A. **Rhetoric:** the art of communicating ideas to audiences in order to facilitate free and rational choices.

    B. **Theory:** a systematic attempt to explain aspects of, or relationships among, phenomena in a given environment or context.

    C. **Rhetorical Theory:** a system of understanding how we can attempt to communicate ideas to audiences in order to facilitate free and rational choices.

II. Elements of a Rhetorical Theory

    A. **Ontology** (What is the nature of reality?)

    B. **Epistemology** or **Praxis** (How does rhetoric work or function?)

    C. **Axiology** (What values should be employed in judging rhetoric?)

III. **Ways to characterize different views of reality**

   A. Stephen Pepper, a scholar in the history of philosophy, wrote a book entitled *World Hypotheses* (1961) which attempted to organize the major philosophical systems of Western civilization into four categories:

   Organicism, Formism, Mechanism, Contextualism. These four categories are a good way to explain the **Ontologies** grounding major rhetorical theories we will discuss in class.

   B. Organicism:

   ➢ mystical, spiritual view of reality

   ➢

   ➢

   ➢

   Example: "the force" from **Star Wars***, "if you build it, they will come" from* **Field of Dreams**

C. Formism:

   ➤ idealistic, critical view of reality

   ➤

   ➤

   ➤

   Example: actual governments are compared to an ideal or utopian government; actual romantic relationships are compared to an ideal relationship

D. Mechanism:

   ➤ scientific view of reality

   ➤

   ➤

   ➤

   Example: automobile mechanic, laboratory scientist

E. Contextualism:

> relativistic view of reality

>

>

>

Example: **Beauty and the Beast**

CHAPTER 1: AN OVERVIEW OF RHETORIC

I. Key Terms

   A. **Symbol:** any mark, sign, sound, or gesture that communicates meaning based on social agreement. Examples?

   B. **Rhetoric:** the systematic study and intentional practice of effective symbolic expression.

   C. **Rhetoric is both an art and a form of discourse:**

      1. As **art,** rhetoric consists of the methods or principles that guide **effective** symbolic expression.

      2. As a **form of discourse,** rhetoric is goal-oriented and seeks, by means of planned use of symbols, to adapt ideas to an audience.

II. Defining Characteristics of Rhetorical Discourse

   A. Rhetoric is **planned:**

   B. Rhetoric **considers the audience,** both imagined and actual:

   C. Rhetoric **reveals human motives** (one's commitments, goals, desires, or purposes when they lead to action):

D. Rhetoric **is a response and invites a response:**

E. Rhetoric **seeks persuasion** through the use of multiple symbolic resources:

    1. Argument:

    2. Appeals:

    3. Arrangement:

    4. Aesthetics:

F. Rhetoric **addresses contingent issues:**

III. **Social Functions of Rhetoric**

    A. Rhetoric **tests ideas:**

B. Rhetoric **assists advocacy:**

C. Rhetoric **distributes power** on a number of different levels, including:

   1. Personal level:

   2. Psychological level:

   3. Political level:

D. Rhetoric **discovers facts** and truths needed for decision-making:

E. Rhetoric **shapes knowledge:**

F. Rhetoric **builds community:**

CHAPTER 2: THE ORIGINS AND EARLY HISTORY OF RHETORIC

I. Origins/Rise of Rhetoric in Ancient Greece

   A. When: 8th–3rd Centuries BC
   B. Where: Mediterranean Basin
   C. Early Indicator: rhetoric in writings of Homer (9th Century BC)
      Three functions of language appear:

      1. Heuristic
      2. Eristic
      3. Protreptic

   D. Why did rhetoric develop in this place at this time?

      1. Economic/geographical factors:

      2. Political factors:

      3. Cultural factors:

II. Emergence of the Sophists

   A. Who were they?

   B. What did they teach?

      1. Truth is relative to time, place, and circumstances. Decisions in both personal behavior and public policy should be based on *endoxa* (premises taken to be probable), rather than revealed truth.

2. Goal of education is development of *arete* (possessing virtue and personal excellence, which is "the ability to manage one's personal affairs in an intelligent manner and to succeed in public" HTR, page 37).

3. *Arete* can be developed through studying a variety of subjects (a little bit of knowledge about a lot of topics) and through the intensive study of **rhetoric.**

C. How did the Sophists teach rhetoric?

D. Why was the sophistic approach to education popular?

E. Why were the Sophists controversial?

 1.

 2.

 3.

 4.

 5. Sophists' view of justice was based on *nomos* (social agreement—whatever was popular at the time), rather than law.

III. **Three Influential Sophists**

de Romilly: "The teaching of both rhetoric and philosophy was marked forever by the ideas that the Sophists introduced and the debates they initiated" (HTR, page 47).

A. Gorgias (485–380 BC)

   1. Background:

   2. Contributions to Rhetoric:

      a. Radical skepticism
      b. Belief in work magic (rhetor as *psychagogos*)

B. Protagoras (485–411 BC)

   1. Background:

   2. Contributions to Rhetoric:

      a. "Man is the measure of all things."
      b. Believed every issue has two sides (pro and con)

C. Isocrates (436–338 BC)

1. Background:

2. Contributions to Rhetoric:

   a. Taught political statesmanship.
   b. Believed rhetorical excellence was a combination of natural talent, extensive training, and education in basic principles.

IV. **Women in Athenian Rhetoric (or lack thereof!)**

A. Aspasia (6th Century BC)

1. Background:

2. Contributions to Rhetoric:

   a. Teacher of Socrates
   b. Speaker and writer

CHAPTER 3 — PLATO VS. THE SOPHISTS: RHETORIC ON TRIAL

PART 1

I. **Plato's Biographical Sketch**

  A. Lived from 427–347 BC
  B. Highly influenced by Socrates, his teacher
  C. Founded **The Academy** in 388 BC
  D. Famous works: *Gorgias* 385 BC, *Phaedrus* 370 BC

II. **Plato's *Gorgias***

  A. Overview and Plot of Dialogue

   ➢ Dialogue: a play written in the style of dialectic
   ➢ Plato argues that Sophistic rhetoric deals in opinion rather than true knowledge
   ➢ Characters: Socrates, Gorgias, Polus, Callicles
   ➢ Dialogue includes three conversations, each between Socrates and a famous Sophist

  B. **Dialogue #1: Socrates and Gorgias** (definition of Sophistic view of rhetoric)

  Overview and Plot of Dialogue

   1. Socrates asks:

    ➢

    ➢

    ➢

    ➢

INTRODUCTION TO RHETORICAL THEORY | 22

2. Gorgias argues:

>

>

>

>

C. **Dialogue #2: Socrates and Polus** (uses of rhetoric)

1. Socrates asks:

>

>

>

2. Polus argues:

>

>

>

D. **Dialogue #3: Socrates and Callicles** (how one should live; Statesman vs. Philosopher)

1. Socrates asks:

    ➤

    ➤

    ➤

2. Callicles argues:

    ➤

    ➤

    ➤

E. In *Gorgias,* Plato raises issues of:

1. **Truth:** absolute truth **versus** opinion about truth.

2. **Audience:** rhetors manipulate their audience **versus** public opinion controls the speaker.

3. **Power:** power as the ability to manipulate others **versus** power self-control grounded in true knowledge of justice.

F. In *Gorgias,* Plato raises 3 questions about rhetoric:

 1. What is the nature of rhetoric (ontology)?

 2. Does rhetoric by its very nature tend to mislead (epistemology)?

 3. What happens to a society when persuasion is a basis for law and justice (axiology)?

G. Outcomes of *Gorgias:*

 1.

 2.

 3.

 4.

H. Is Plato fair to rhetoric?

True Arts of Health

Body: gymnastics   (maintain)
              medicine   (restore)

Soul: legislation   (maintain)
              justice   (restore)

Sham Arts of Health

Body: make-up   (maintain)
              cookery   (restore)

Soul: sophistic   (maintain)
              rhetoric   (restore)

PART 3

PHAEDRUS PAGES 60-64

III. Plato's *Phaedrus*

  A. Overview and plot of dialogue

   - Written about 15 years after *Gorgias*
   - Contains more hopeful statements about the possibility of a "just" rhetoric
   - Characters: Socrates, Phaedrus (student), and Lysias (orator)
   - Dialogue has two parts:

     Part I: 3 *allegorical speeches* about "love"
     Part II: Elements of an *ideal rhetoric*

  B. Part I: 3 *allegorical speeches* about "love"
     "Love" = persuasion, communication, or relationship between speaker and audience

   Speech #1: The "Non-Lover"
   Phaedrus' interpretation of Lysias' speech.

   Topic: "Being a non-lover is better than being a lover."

   Meaning: Persuasion should involve neutral, semantically pure communication, a medium of exchange that avoids value judgments.

   Socrates rejects this.

Speech #2: The "Evil Lover"
Socrates' interpretation of Lysias' speech.

Topic: "Being a lover is better than being a non-lover."

Meaning: Persuasion can involve the use of emotional language, deception or distortion by the speaker as tools to control or dominate that audience.

Socrates rejects this.

Speech #3: The "Noble Lover"
Socrates' view on true love.

Topic: Authentic love is a form of "divine madness" in which each person thinks of the other's well-being above their own.

Meaning: Authentic or "true" persuasion occurs when a speaker acts as a noble lover, addressing the souls of the audience in order to move them toward the Good.

Socrates' views: "myth of the charioteer"

The 3 Souls:

C. Part II: Elements of an *ideal rhetoric*

A good rhetorician must be:

- A **philosopher** who knows the "truth" of the subject.
- A **logician** who can define and organize items.
- An **organizer** who can arrange speech materials so that the speech resembles a living creature.
- A **psychologist** who understands and adapts to the souls of the audience.
- A **good speaker** who can influence through style and delivery.
- A **humble individual** who recognizes inherent limitations of writing and public speaking.
- A **just person** with a high moral purpose.

CHAPTER 4   ARISTOTLE ON RHETORIC

PART 1

PAGES 69-75

I. **Biographical Notes**

   A. Lived from 384–322 BC

   B. Born in northern Greece, came to Athens in 367 BC

   C. Studied at Plato's academy for 20 years; scientific background

   D. Established Lyceum in 335 BC

   E. Wrote hundreds of books on variety of subjects: mathematics, politics, ethics, physics, zoology

II. **Ontology**

   A.

   B.

   C.

III. **Aristotle's *Rhetoric***

   Series of lecture notes compiled by his students into three books:

   Book I: *Definition of Rhetoric and Types of Speeches*

   Book II: *Rhetorical Proofs: Ethos, Pathos, Logos*

   Book III: *Style, Arrangement, and Delivery*

IV. Differences between Plato and Aristotle (outline)

V. Definition, Uses, and Forms of Rhetoric

   A. What is the difference between Rhetoric and Dialectic?

      1.

      2.

      3.

      4.

   B. Definition of Rhetoric:

C. Rhetoric as a Techne (true art)

   1. Rhetoric has its own domain—subject matter.

   2. Rhetoric functions to "discover the means" rather than solely to succeed in persuasion.

   3. Even if you are unsuccessful, you can still use rhetoric as a techne.

D. Four uses of Rhetoric:

   1.

   2.

   3.

   4.

E. Enthymeme as a Form of Argument:

PART 2

PAGES 75–84

VI. Epistemology

VII. Three Rhetorical Settings
      Rhetoric Book 1, Chapters 4–15

TYPE OF SPEECH	CONTEXT	PURPOSE	TIME ORIENTATION	SUBJECTS COVERED/ MESSAGES CONVEYED
Deliberative				
Ceremonial (or epideictic)				
Forensic				

Examples:

VIII. **Types of Artistic Proof**

    A. Inartistic Proofs:

    B. Artistic Proofs:

        1. Logos:

        2. Ethos:

        3. Pathos:

PART 3

SUPPLEMENTAL MATERIAL

IX. **Aristotle's Axiology**

    A. Based on Concept of *Values:*

    B. Aristotle's Conception of *The Good:*

        1. Individual Good:

        2. Societal Good:

    C. Aristotle's Conception of *Justice:*

        1. Two (2) Kinds of Laws: *Specific* and *Universal*

        2. Justice Should Be Based on Equity

CHAPTER 5 — RHETORIC AT ROME: CICERO

I. **Roman Society and a Place for Rhetoric:**

   A. Systems of Government changed.

   B. Rhetoric was central to Roman education.

II. **Marcus Tullius Cicero: Biographical Notes:**

   - Born January 3, 106 BC; Dies 43 BCE
   - Lower tier Aristocratic Family
   - Became Lawyer

   A. Wrote *De Inventione* at age 19: musings on Greek and Roman Republic Rhetoric

   - Union of Wisdom and Eloquence:

   - Canons of Rhetoric:

   - Stasis and Loci: Judicial Argument:

B. He later wrote *De Oratore:* Mature work written in response to Plato's *Gorgias*.

➢ Reinforced the Union of Wisdom and Eloquence:

➢ Audience Centrality:

III. **The Second Sophistic Refers to a Change in Government**

A. Government reverted back to an Empire where free speech was frowned upon.

B. The role of rhetoric again changed.

CHAPTER 6: RHETORIC IN CHRISTIAN EUROPE: ST. AUGUSTINE

I. **St. Augustine Emerged as a Leader of Rhetoric—353–430 CE**

   A. Born in Hippo, Northern Africa.

   B. Well educated in rhetoric—Cicero style.

   C. A well-known professor of rhetoric.

   D. Wrote *Confessions* upon his conversion to Christianity.

   E. Wrote *On Christian Doctrine* as a Guide to Preaching.

II. **The Fall of the Roman Empire Brought Rhetoric to Christian Europe**

   A. This period is referred to as The Middle Ages.
      1. Rhetoric declined after conquests:

      2. The classical Greek tradition:

3. Reminiscent of the Second Sophistic:

B. The Church came into power.

III. Ontology: Pagan or Scriptural philosophy of rhetoric?

IV. Epistemology: Wrote *On Christian Doctrine*

V. Axiology: A search for Truth?

CHAPTER 9 — CONTEMPORARY RHETORIC I: ARGUMENT, AUDIENCES, AND ADVOCACY

JURGEN HABERMAS: RHETORIC IN THE PUBLIC SPHERE

I. **Habermas: Biographical Sketch**

    A. Born in Germany in 1929.

    B. Deeply affected by WWII.

    C. Graduate student at Frankfurt School (1940s).

    D. Professor at Frankfurt School (1960s).

Chapter 9 — CONTEMPORARY RHETORIC I: ARGUMENT, AUDIENCES, AND ADVOCACY

II. A Rational Society

III. What is the Public Sphere?

IV. Criteria for Participation in Public Sphere

CHAPTER 10 — CONTEMPORARY RHETORIC II: KENNETH BURKE

PART 1: THE RHETORIC OF DRAMA: KENNETH BURKE

PAGES 209–214 & BURKE BIOGRAPHY POSTED ON BB & READING BY DAVID LING SUPPLEMENT POSTED ON BB

I. **Understanding Kenneth Burke**

   A. Biographical Sketch:

   - Northerner
   - Dropped out of School
   - Associated with Communism
   - Literary Critic, Philosopher, Liberal
   - "Foremost rhetorician of the 20th century" (Golden, 312).
   - Difficult theory to understand: eclectic, makes up new terms, unorganized.

   B. Major Works:

   - *Philosophy of Literary Form* (1941)
   - *A Grammar of Motives* (1945)
   - *A Rhetoric of Motives* (1950)

II. **Ontology**

   A. All Humans are Symbolic Interactionists (constructionist):

   1. Experience = interaction between realms of physical motion and symbolic action:

2. Human Being = five fold definition:

>

>

>

>

>

3. Language shapes human experience through:

   a. Use of Terministic Screens:

B. View of human society/experience = **Dramatism:**

   1. Human society is characterized by constant merger and division of groups based on motives.

   2. As groups struggle to obtain resources and status in accordance with their purposes, they enact roles and interact in dramatic ways:

   3. Individuals and groups use symbolic action—rhetoric—as the primary instrument to induce cooperation and to serve their own purposes.

III. **How rhetoric should be judged: Axiology**

   A. For speakers: "The good life": maximum physicality, peaceful cooperation, free expression, charity.

B. For audiences: development of critical consciousness.

IV. Contributions to rhetorical theory: Epistemology

   A. **Definition of Rhetoric:**

   Expanded the way we study rhetoric in 3 ways:

   1. Rhetoric persuades the speaker as well in the audience.

   2. Rhetoric can work at both conscious and unconscious levels.

   3. All human symbolic activity includes a rhetorical (persuasive) dimension.

   B. **Lines of argument:** strategies used to induce cooperation:

   1. Identification:

   2. Transcendence:

C. **Dramatistic Pentad:** Vocabulary of critical terms that identifies motives of the speaker by examining their language and how they define situations.

1. Act:

2. Scene:

3. Agent:

4. Agency:

5. Purpose:

*Terms **can** be paired into ratios that provide the basis for defining a situation.
*Ratios = relationship among terms of the pentad

PART 2: THE RHETORICAL SITUATION: LLOYD BITZER
PAGES 215-217 & READING BY SMITH POSTED ON BB

I. **Introduction**

    A. Lloyd Bitzer's situational model is unique.

        1. We need to develop an understanding of his theory.

        2. We need to evaluate/apply this theory to the definition of a rhetorical theory.

II. **Definitions**

    A. Bitzer's theory of Rhetorical Situation:

        1. Definition of Rhetorical Situation:

        2. Examples:

    B. There are **3** components to the theory:

        1. Exigence:

        2. Audience:

3. Constraints:

C. Characteristics of Bitzer's Theory:

III. How does Bitzer's theory of rhetorical situation include the necessary elements of a rhetorical theory?

  A. Ontology:

  B. Epistemology:

  C. Axiology:

IV. Using the 3 components of Bitzer's theory, let's analyze Bush's speech on the "War on Drugs."

- Audience #1 = American Public
- Audience #2 = Junior high and high schoolers
- Bush's appeal was successful in convincing the public that "the drug crisis" was one of the most important problems facing the country and strengthened support for Bush by middle and upper class Americans.

    A. Exigence:

    B. Audience:

    C. Constraints:

Chapter 10 | CONTEMPORARY RHETORIC II: KENNETH BURKE

LECTURE: THE MYTH OF THE RHETORICAL SITUATION: RICHARD VATZ
READING SUPPLEMENT POSTED ON BB

I. Richard Vatz: "The Myth of the Rhetorical Situation" was written as a response to Lloyd Bitzer's "Rhetorical Situation."

   A. What is the "Myth" that Vatz refers to in his article?

   B. How is his stance on rhetoric different from Bitzer's?

II. **Ontology:** Meaning is not found in events, facts, people, or "situations," nor are facts "publicly observable."

III. **Epistemology:** Communication of events is a two-part process:

   A.

   B.

IV. **Axiology:** Quality of the rhetoric rests with:

V. **A Contrast of the Bitzer/Vatz View of Rhetoric**

   Bitzer   **Vatz**

   1. Rhetoric is situational.   1.

   2. Exigence strongly invites utterance.   2.

   3. Situation controls the R's Response.   3.

   4. Rhetoric obtains its character from the   4.
      situation which generates it.

PART 3: RHETORIC AS NARRATION: BAHKTIN & BORMANN
PAGES 217-220 & BORMANN READING SUPPLEMENT POSTED ON BB

I. Michael Bahktin: Biographical Sketch

> Lived from 1895–1975
> Grew up in Communist Russia

II. Polyphonic Novel

   A. Questioned the objectivity of discourse:

   1. Language use is inherently social.

   2. Language use is inherently ideological.

   3. Language use is inherently dialogic.

   B. Social World is made up of multiple positions or "voices."

   1. Rhetoricians should examine dialogues "chains of assertion and response" to determine various voices they contain and identify or "free" the voices that are overlooked or marginalized.

   2. The best version is public discussion or writing that allows equal voice to varied perspectives within a community.

3. Truth is the process of dialogic negotiation.

III. **Ernest Bormann: Biographical Sketch**

   ➢ Lived from 1925–2008
   ➢ Taught at the University of Minnesota
   ➢ Studied Business Organizations

IV. **Role of Narration**

   A. Rhetorical narratives play a role in shaping community and culture.

      1. Narratives establish commonly held meanings among people.

      2. Communication = process of developing or 'chaining out' narratives within groups.

      3. Symbolic convergence = converging of viewpoints or 'symbolic worlds.'

   B. Fantasy Themes

      1. Fantasy = a story shared by a group

2. Fantasy theme = a story line involving characters and a plot

3. Narrative structures of a **fantasy theme:**

    ➤ Inside joke:

    ➤ Fantasy type:

    ➤ Rhetorical vision:

    ➤ Organizational sage:

LECTURE: RHETORIC, POWER, AND SOCIAL CRITICISM: RICHARD WEAVER

READING SUPPLEMENT POSTED ON BB

I. **Understanding Richard Weaver**

   A. Background: (pages 55–59)

   - Southerner: Anti-Modernist
   - Teacher
   - Philosopher
   - Conservative

   B. Major Works:

   - *Ideas Have Consequences* (1948)
   - *The Ethics of Rhetoric* (1953)
   - *Visions of Order* (1964)

II. **Ontology: Believed in universal forms (pages 59–61)**

   A. View of Humans

   - Human = body + mind + soul

   - Mind = emotional + ethical + religious + rational

   - Soul: guides mind and body

B. Rational Capacity includes three orders of knowledge:

   1. Facts ("ideas")

   2. Statements about facts ("beliefs")

   3. Statements about statements ("metaphysical dream")

IV. Axiology: "The Good" (pages 61–63, 74–78)

   A. The goal of rhetoric should be to promote "the Good," especially a return to the values preferred by Weaver.

   B. Weaver's preferred values—tradition, civility, peace, justice, cultural diversity, stability, order—are being threatened by **progress,** the tyrannizing image of the modern era.

   C. Every culture has a value system embodied in a "tyrannizing image," a cultural ideal or vision of excellence for which a society strives.

IV. **Contributions to rhetorical theory: Epistemology**

   A. Relationship between rhetoric and dialectic (pages 63–65)

   1. Dialectic is "method of investigation whose object is the establishment of truth about doubtful propositions" (p. 63). Involves proper arrangement of data into orders of knowledge (facts, statements about facts, statements about statements).

   2. Rhetoric is *the persuading of human beings to adopt right attitudes and act in relation to them.*

   3. **Ethical persuasion** involves a combination of rhetoric **and** dialectic.

      a. Dialectic alone cannot move people; it's too abstract to consider real world situations.

      b. Rhetoric alone can be perverted to the use of base techniques in the service of evil ends.

      c. Conclusion: "There is, then, no true rhetoric without dialectic." (1953, 17)

B. Five lines of argument (pages 66–70)

   1. **Genus or Definition:** an argument based on the nature of the thing, on its essential and unchanging properties. STRONGEST. Argument of the conservative.

   2. **Similitude:** an argument based on comparison or analogy between properties of two similar things.

   3. **Cause & Effect or Consequence:** an argument based on cause-effect; "X" should be chosen or avoided because it leads to "Y." WEAKEST. Argument of the liberal.

   4. **Authority:** an argument based on the testimony of external sources.

   5. **Rhetorical-Historical:** an argument that combines definition with context.

C. Ultimate terms (pages 73–74)

1. Source: Human need for order, order in culture is determined by "tyrannizing image," including language.

2. **Terms** are names capable of entering into propositions. Terms exist in rhetorical chains leading toward **ultimate** terms.

3. **God Term:** an expression below which all others are ranked as subordinate. Term carries ultimate positive sanction.

    1953: "progress"   2016–17:

4. **Devil Term:** an expression that stands at the end of a series as the prime repellent. Term carries ultimate negative sanction.

    1953: "Communist"   2016–17:

5. **Charismatic Term:** an expression of considerable potency gained by social convention rather than connection to history or philosophy.

    1953: "freedom"   2016–17:

D. "Language as sermonic" (pages 65–66)

1. Since all language contains implied values and all language has the potential to persuade others, speakers should take responsibility for their rhetorical choices.

2. Examples: racist, sexist language (use of ultimate terms)

CHAPTER 11 — CONTEMPORARY RHETORIC III: TEXTS, POWER, AND ALTERNATIVES

FEMINISM & RHETORIC: CRITIQUE AND REFORM

PAGES 238-243 & 2 READING SUPPLEMENTS POSTED ON BB

I. Definitions:

   A. Feminism is the belief that "men and women should have equal opportunity for self-expression" (Foss, 1989, page 151).

   B. A feminist perspective:

      1. "is designed to analyze and evaluate the use of rhetoric to construct and maintain particular gender definitions for women and men" (Foss, 151).

      2. is designed to question the focus on male rhetoric in rhetorical theory.

II. Assumptions:

   A. Gender is culturally constructed through language and symbols that contribute to the exclusion of women's experience and voices in our society.

   B. Women experience the world differently than men do.

C. Rhetorical practices and rhetorical theory reflect male experiences in ways of understanding and labeling that experience.

III. Reform: Toward a New Model:

    A. **Conversion Model:** the goal of rhetoric is to convert others to one's own view.

       Examples:

    B. **Invitational Model:** the goal of rhetoric does not require a persuasive intent on the part of the speaker.

       Examples: